WEBSITE: _____

EMAIL: _____

USERNAME: _____

PASSWORD(S): _____

_____

_____

NOTES/SECURITY QUESTIONS/PINS: _____

_____

WEBSITE: _____

EMAIL: _____

USERNAME: _____

PASSWORD(S): _____

_____

_____

NOTES/SECURITY QUESTIONS/PINS: _____

_____

_____

WEBSITE: _____

EMAIL: _____

USERNAME: _____

PASSWORD(S): _____

_____

_____

NOTES/SECURITY QUESTIONS/PINS: _____

_____

_____

A

WEBSITE: _____

EMAIL: _____

USERNAME: _____

PASSWORD(S): _____

_____

_____

NOTES/SECURITY QUESTIONS/PINS: _____

_____

_____

WEBSITE: _____

EMAIL: _____

USERNAME: _____

PASSWORD(S): _____

_____

_____

NOTES/SECURITY QUESTIONS/PINS: _____

_____

_____

_____

WEBSITE: _____

EMAIL: _____

USERNAME: _____

PASSWORD(S): _____

_____

_____

NOTES/SECURITY QUESTIONS/PINS: _____

_____

_____

WEBSITE:

EMAIL:

USERNAME:

PASSWORD(S):

NOTES/SECURITY QUESTIONS/PINS:

WEBSITE:

EMAIL:

USERNAME:

PASSWORD(S):

NOTES/SECURITY QUESTIONS/PINS:

WEBSITE:

EMAIL:

USERNAME:

PASSWORD(S):

NOTES/SECURITY QUESTIONS/PINS:

A

WEBSITE:

EMAIL:

USERNAME:

PASSWORD(S):

NOTES/SECURITY QUESTIONS/PINS:

WEBSITE:

EMAIL:

USERNAME:

PASSWORD(S):

NOTES/SECURITY QUESTIONS/PINS:

WEBSITE:

EMAIL:

USERNAME:

PASSWORD(S):

NOTES/SECURITY QUESTIONS/PINS:

WEBSITE:

EMAIL:

USERNAME:

PASSWORD(S):

NOTES/SECURITY QUESTIONS/PINS:

WEBSITE:

EMAIL:

USERNAME:

PASSWORD(S):

NOTES/SECURITY QUESTIONS/PINS:

WEBSITE:

EMAIL:

USERNAME:

PASSWORD(S):

NOTES/SECURITY QUESTIONS/PINS:

B

WEBSITE:

EMAIL:

USERNAME:

PASSWORD(S):

NOTES/SECURITY QUESTIONS/PINS:

WEBSITE:

EMAIL:

USERNAME:

PASSWORD(S):

NOTES/SECURITY QUESTIONS/PINS:

WEBSITE:

EMAIL:

USERNAME:

PASSWORD(S):

NOTES/SECURITY QUESTIONS/PINS:

WEBSITE:

EMAIL:

USERNAME:

PASSWORD(S):

NOTES/SECURITY QUESTIONS/PINS:

WEBSITE:

EMAIL:

USERNAME:

PASSWORD(S):

NOTES/SECURITY QUESTIONS/PINS:

WEBSITE:

EMAIL:

USERNAME:

PASSWORD(S):

NOTES/SECURITY QUESTIONS/PINS:

B

WEBSITE:

EMAIL:

USERNAME:

PASSWORD(S):

NOTES/SECURITY QUESTIONS/PINS:

WEBSITE:

EMAIL:

USERNAME:

PASSWORD(S):

NOTES/SECURITY QUESTIONS/PINS:

WEBSITE:

EMAIL:

USERNAME:

PASSWORD(S):

NOTES/SECURITY QUESTIONS/PINS:

WEBSITE:

EMAIL:

USERNAME:

PASSWORD(S):

NOTES/SECURITY QUESTIONS/PINS:

WEBSITE:

EMAIL:

USERNAME:

PASSWORD(S):

NOTES/SECURITY QUESTIONS/PINS:

WEBSITE:

EMAIL:

USERNAME:

PASSWORD(S):

NOTES/SECURITY QUESTIONS/PINS:

WEBSITE:

EMAIL:

G USERNAME:

PASSWORD(S):

NOTES/SECURITY QUESTIONS/PINS:

WEBSITE:

EMAIL:

USERNAME:

PASSWORD(S):

NOTES/SECURITY QUESTIONS/PINS:

WEBSITE:

EMAIL:

USERNAME:

PASSWORD(S):

NOTES/SECURITY QUESTIONS/PINS:

WEBSITE:

EMAIL:

C

USERNAME:

PASSWORD(S):

NOTES/SECURITY QUESTIONS/PINS:

WEBSITE:

EMAIL:

USERNAME:

PASSWORD(S):

NOTES/SECURITY QUESTIONS/PINS:

WEBSITE:

EMAIL:

USERNAME:

PASSWORD(S):

NOTES/SECURITY QUESTIONS/PINS:

WEBSITE:

EMAIL:

C USERNAME:

PASSWORD(S):

_____

_____

NOTES/SECURITY QUESTIONS/PINS:

_____

WEBSITE:

EMAIL:

USERNAME:

PASSWORD(S):

_____

_____

NOTES/SECURITY QUESTIONS/PINS:

_____

_____

WEBSITE:

EMAIL:

USERNAME:

PASSWORD(S):

_____

_____

NOTES/SECURITY QUESTIONS/PINS:

_____

_____

WEBSITE:

EMAIL:

USERNAME:

PASSWORD(S):

NOTES/SECURITY QUESTIONS/PINS:

WEBSITE:

EMAIL:

USERNAME:

PASSWORD(S):

NOTES/SECURITY QUESTIONS/PINS:

WEBSITE:

EMAIL:

USERNAME:

PASSWORD(S):

NOTES/SECURITY QUESTIONS/PINS:

WEBSITE:

EMAIL:

USERNAME:

PASSWORD(S):

NOTES/SECURITY QUESTIONS/PINS:

WEBSITE:

EMAIL:

USERNAME:

PASSWORD(S):

NOTES/SECURITY QUESTIONS/PINS:

WEBSITE:

EMAIL:

USERNAME:

PASSWORD(S):

NOTES/SECURITY QUESTIONS/PINS:

WEBSITE:

EMAIL:

USERNAME:

PASSWORD(S):

NOTES/SECURITY QUESTIONS/PINS:

WEBSITE:

EMAIL:

USERNAME:

PASSWORD(S):

NOTES/SECURITY QUESTIONS/PINS:

WEBSITE:

EMAIL:

USERNAME:

PASSWORD(S):

NOTES/SECURITY QUESTIONS/PINS:

WEBSITE:

EMAIL:

USERNAME:

PASSWORD(S):

NOTES/SECURITY QUESTIONS/PINS:

WEBSITE:

EMAIL:

USERNAME:

PASSWORD(S):

NOTES/SECURITY QUESTIONS/PINS:

WEBSITE:

EMAIL:

USERNAME:

PASSWORD(S):

NOTES/SECURITY QUESTIONS/PINS:

WEBSITE:

EMAIL:

USERNAME:

PASSWORD(S):

_ε_

NOTES/SECURITY QUESTIONS/PINS:

WEBSITE:

EMAIL:

USERNAME:

PASSWORD(S):

NOTES/SECURITY QUESTIONS/PINS:

WEBSITE:

EMAIL:

USERNAME:

PASSWORD(S):

NOTES/SECURITY QUESTIONS/PINS:

WEBSITE:

EMAIL:

USERNAME:

PASSWORD(S):

NOTES/SECURITY QUESTIONS/PINS:

WEBSITE:

EMAIL:

USERNAME:

PASSWORD(S):

NOTES/SECURITY QUESTIONS/PINS:

WEBSITE:

EMAIL:

USERNAME:

PASSWORD(S):

NOTES/SECURITY QUESTIONS/PINS:

WEBSITE:

EMAIL:

USERNAME:

PASSWORD(S):

ε

NOTES/SECURITY QUESTIONS/PINS:

WEBSITE:

EMAIL:

USERNAME:

PASSWORD(S):

NOTES/SECURITY QUESTIONS/PINS:

WEBSITE:

EMAIL:

USERNAME:

PASSWORD(S):

NOTES/SECURITY QUESTIONS/PINS:

WEBSITE:

EMAIL:

USERNAME:

PASSWORD(S):

NOTES/SECURITY QUESTIONS/PINS:

WEBSITE:

EMAIL:

USERNAME:

PASSWORD(S):

NOTES/SECURITY QUESTIONS/PINS:

WEBSITE:

EMAIL:

USERNAME:

PASSWORD(S):

NOTES/SECURITY QUESTIONS/PINS:

WEBSITE:

EMAIL:

USERNAME:

PASSWORD(S):

F

NOTES/SECURITY QUESTIONS/PINS:

WEBSITE:

EMAIL:

USERNAME:

PASSWORD(S):

NOTES/SECURITY QUESTIONS/PINS:

WEBSITE:

EMAIL:

USERNAME:

PASSWORD(S):

NOTES/SECURITY QUESTIONS/PINS:

WEBSITE:

EMAIL:

USERNAME:

PASSWORD(S):

F

NOTES/SECURITY QUESTIONS/PINS:

WEBSITE:

EMAIL:

USERNAME:

PASSWORD(S):

NOTES/SECURITY QUESTIONS/PINS:

WEBSITE:

EMAIL:

USERNAME:

PASSWORD(S):

NOTES/SECURITY QUESTIONS/PINS:

WEBSITE:

EMAIL:

USERNAME:

PASSWORD(S):

_____ F

NOTES/SECURITY QUESTIONS/PINS:

WEBSITE:

EMAIL:

USERNAME:

PASSWORD(S):

NOTES/SECURITY QUESTIONS/PINS:

WEBSITE:

EMAIL:

USERNAME:

PASSWORD(S):

NOTES/SECURITY QUESTIONS/PINS:

WEBSITE:

EMAIL:

USERNAME:

PASSWORD(S):

F

NOTES/SECURITY QUESTIONS/PINS:

WEBSITE:

EMAIL:

USERNAME:

PASSWORD(S):

NOTES/SECURITY QUESTIONS/PINS:

WEBSITE:

EMAIL:

USERNAME:

PASSWORD(S):

NOTES/SECURITY QUESTIONS/PINS:

WEBSITE:

EMAIL:

USERNAME:

PASSWORD(S):

NOTES/SECURITY QUESTIONS/PINS:

G

WEBSITE:

EMAIL:

USERNAME:

PASSWORD(S):

NOTES/SECURITY QUESTIONS/PINS:

WEBSITE:

EMAIL:

USERNAME:

PASSWORD(S):

NOTES/SECURITY QUESTIONS/PINS:

WEBSITE:

EMAIL:

USERNAME:

PASSWORD(S):

G NOTES/SECURITY QUESTIONS/PINS:

WEBSITE:

EMAIL:

USERNAME:

PASSWORD(S):

NOTES/SECURITY QUESTIONS/PINS:

WEBSITE:

EMAIL:

USERNAME:

PASSWORD(S):

NOTES/SECURITY QUESTIONS/PINS:

WEBSITE:

EMAIL:

USERNAME:

PASSWORD(S):

NOTES/SECURITY QUESTIONS/PINS: *G*

WEBSITE:

EMAIL:

USERNAME:

PASSWORD(S):

NOTES/SECURITY QUESTIONS/PINS:

WEBSITE:

EMAIL:

USERNAME:

PASSWORD(S):

NOTES/SECURITY QUESTIONS/PINS:

WEBSITE:

EMAIL:

USERNAME:

PASSWORD(S):

G NOTES/SECURITY QUESTIONS/PINS:

WEBSITE:

EMAIL:

USERNAME:

PASSWORD(S):

NOTES/SECURITY QUESTIONS/PINS:

WEBSITE:

EMAIL:

USERNAME:

PASSWORD(S):

NOTES/SECURITY QUESTIONS/PINS:

WEBSITE:

EMAIL:

USERNAME:

PASSWORD(S):

NOTES/SECURITY QUESTIONS/PINS:

WEBSITE:

EMAIL:

USERNAME:

PASSWORD(S):

NOTES/SECURITY QUESTIONS/PINS:

WEBSITE:

EMAIL:

USERNAME:

PASSWORD(S):

NOTES/SECURITY QUESTIONS/PINS:

WEBSITE:

EMAIL:

USERNAME:

PASSWORD(S):

NOTES/SECURITY QUESTIONS/PINS:

WEBSITE:

EMAIL:

USERNAME:

PASSWORD(S):

NOTES/SECURITY QUESTIONS/PINS:

WEBSITE:

EMAIL:

USERNAME:

PASSWORD(S):

NOTES/SECURITY QUESTIONS/PINS:

WEBSITE:

EMAIL:

USERNAME:

PASSWORD(S):

NOTES/SECURITY QUESTIONS/PINS:

H

WEBSITE:

EMAIL:

USERNAME:

PASSWORD(S):

NOTES/SECURITY QUESTIONS/PINS:

WEBSITE:

EMAIL:

USERNAME:

PASSWORD(S):

NOTES/SECURITY QUESTIONS/PINS:

WEBSITE:

EMAIL:

USERNAME:

PASSWORD(S):

NOTES/SECURITY QUESTIONS/PINS:

H

WEBSITE:

EMAIL:

USERNAME:

PASSWORD(S):

NOTES/SECURITY QUESTIONS/PINS:

WEBSITE:

EMAIL:

USERNAME:

PASSWORD(S):

NOTES/SECURITY QUESTIONS/PINS:

WEBSITE:

EMAIL:

USERNAME:

PASSWORD(S):

NOTES/SECURITY QUESTIONS/PINS:

I

WEBSITE:

EMAIL:

USERNAME:

PASSWORD(S):

NOTES/SECURITY QUESTIONS/PINS:

WEBSITE:

EMAIL:

USERNAME:

PASSWORD(S):

NOTES/SECURITY QUESTIONS/PINS:

WEBSITE:

EMAIL:

USERNAME:

PASSWORD(S):

NOTES/SECURITY QUESTIONS/PINS:

WEBSITE:

EMAIL:

USERNAME:

PASSWORD(S):

NOTES/SECURITY QUESTIONS/PINS:

WEBSITE:

EMAIL:

USERNAME:

PASSWORD(S):

NOTES/SECURITY QUESTIONS/PINS:

WEBSITE: _____

EMAIL: _____

USERNAME: _____

PASSWORD(S): _____

_____

_____

NOTES/SECURITY QUESTIONS/PINS: _____

_____

WEBSITE: _____

EMAIL: _____

USERNAME: _____

PASSWORD(S): _____

_____

_____

NOTES/SECURITY QUESTIONS/PINS: _____

_____

_____

_____

WEBSITE: _____

EMAIL: _____

USERNAME: _____

PASSWORD(S): _____

_____

_____

NOTES/SECURITY QUESTIONS/PINS: _____

_____

_____

WEBSITE:

EMAIL:

USERNAME:

PASSWORD(S):

NOTES/SECURITY QUESTIONS/PINS:

I

WEBSITE:

EMAIL:

USERNAME:

PASSWORD(S):

NOTES/SECURITY QUESTIONS/PINS:

WEBSITE:

EMAIL:

USERNAME:

PASSWORD(S):

NOTES/SECURITY QUESTIONS/PINS:

WEBSITE:

EMAIL:

USERNAME:

PASSWORD(S):

NOTES/SECURITY QUESTIONS/PINS:

J

WEBSITE:

EMAIL:

USERNAME:

PASSWORD(S):

NOTES/SECURITY QUESTIONS/PINS:

WEBSITE:

EMAIL:

USERNAME:

PASSWORD(S):

NOTES/SECURITY QUESTIONS/PINS:

WEBSITE:

EMAIL:

USERNAME:

PASSWORD(S):

NOTES/SECURITY QUESTIONS/PINS:

J WEBSITE:

EMAIL:

USERNAME:

PASSWORD(S):

NOTES/SECURITY QUESTIONS/PINS:

WEBSITE:

EMAIL:

USERNAME:

PASSWORD(S):

NOTES/SECURITY QUESTIONS/PINS:

WEBSITE:

EMAIL:

USERNAME:

PASSWORD(S):

NOTES/SECURITY QUESTIONS/PINS:

J

WEBSITE:

EMAIL:

USERNAME:

PASSWORD(S):

NOTES/SECURITY QUESTIONS/PINS:

WEBSITE:

EMAIL:

USERNAME:

PASSWORD(S):

NOTES/SECURITY QUESTIONS/PINS:

WEBSITE:

EMAIL:

USERNAME:

PASSWORD(S):

NOTES/SECURITY QUESTIONS/PINS:

J WEBSITE:

EMAIL:

USERNAME:

PASSWORD(S):

NOTES/SECURITY QUESTIONS/PINS:

WEBSITE:

EMAIL:

USERNAME:

PASSWORD(S):

NOTES/SECURITY QUESTIONS/PINS:

WEBSITE:

EMAIL:

USERNAME:

PASSWORD(S):

NOTES/SECURITY QUESTIONS/PINS:

WEBSITE:

EMAIL:

USERNAME:

PASSWORD(S):

NOTES/SECURITY QUESTIONS/PINS:

WEBSITE:

EMAIL:

USERNAME:

PASSWORD(S):

NOTES/SECURITY QUESTIONS/PINS:

WEBSITE:

EMAIL:

USERNAME:

PASSWORD(S):

NOTES/SECURITY QUESTIONS/PINS:

WEBSITE:

k EMAIL:

USERNAME:

PASSWORD(S):

NOTES/SECURITY QUESTIONS/PINS:

WEBSITE:

EMAIL:

USERNAME:

PASSWORD(S):

NOTES/SECURITY QUESTIONS/PINS:

WEBSITE:

EMAIL:

USERNAME:

PASSWORD(S):

NOTES/SECURITY QUESTIONS/PINS:

WEBSITE:

EMAIL:

USERNAME:

PASSWORD(S):

NOTES/SECURITY QUESTIONS/PINS:

WEBSITE:

EMAIL:

USERNAME:

PASSWORD(S):

NOTES/SECURITY QUESTIONS/PINS:

WEBSITE:

EMAIL:

USERNAME:

PASSWORD(S):

NOTES/SECURITY QUESTIONS/PINS:

WEBSITE:

k EMAIL:

USERNAME:

PASSWORD(S):

NOTES/SECURITY QUESTIONS/PINS:

WEBSITE:

EMAIL:

USERNAME:

PASSWORD(S):

NOTES/SECURITY QUESTIONS/PINS:

WEBSITE:

EMAIL:

USERNAME:

PASSWORD(S):

NOTES/SECURITY QUESTIONS/PINS:

WEBSITE:

EMAIL:

USERNAME:

PASSWORD(S):

NOTES/SECURITY QUESTIONS/PINS:

WEBSITE:

EMAIL:

USERNAME:

PASSWORD(S):

NOTES/SECURITY QUESTIONS/PINS:

WEBSITE:

EMAIL:

USERNAME:

PASSWORD(S):

NOTES/SECURITY QUESTIONS/PINS:

WEBSITE:

EMAIL:

USERNAME:

PASSWORD(S):

NOTES/SECURITY QUESTIONS/PINS:

WEBSITE:

EMAIL:

USERNAME:

PASSWORD(S):

NOTES/SECURITY QUESTIONS/PINS:

WEBSITE:

EMAIL:

USERNAME:

PASSWORD(S):

NOTES/SECURITY QUESTIONS/PINS:

WEBSITE:

EMAIL:

USERNAME:

PASSWORD(S):

NOTES/SECURITY QUESTIONS/PINS:

WEBSITE:

EMAIL:

USERNAME:

PASSWORD(S):

NOTES/SECURITY QUESTIONS/PINS:

WEBSITE:

EMAIL:

USERNAME:

PASSWORD(S):

NOTES/SECURITY QUESTIONS/PINS:

WEBSITE:

EMAIL:

USERNAME:

PASSWORD(S):

NOTES/SECURITY QUESTIONS/PINS:

WEBSITE:

EMAIL:

USERNAME:

PASSWORD(S):

NOTES/SECURITY QUESTIONS/PINS:

WEBSITE:

EMAIL:

USERNAME:

PASSWORD(S):

NOTES/SECURITY QUESTIONS/PINS:

WEBSITE:

EMAIL:

USERNAME:

PASSWORD(S):

NOTES/SECURITY QUESTIONS/PINS:

WEBSITE:

EMAIL:

USERNAME:

PASSWORD(S):

NOTES/SECURITY QUESTIONS/PINS:

WEBSITE:

EMAIL:

USERNAME:

PASSWORD(S):

NOTES/SECURITY QUESTIONS/PINS:

WEBSITE:

EMAIL:

USERNAME:

M PASSWORD(S):

NOTES/SECURITY QUESTIONS/PINS:

WEBSITE:

EMAIL:

USERNAME:

PASSWORD(S):

NOTES/SECURITY QUESTIONS/PINS:

WEBSITE:

EMAIL:

USERNAME:

PASSWORD(S):

NOTES/SECURITY QUESTIONS/PINS:

WEBSITE:

EMAIL:

USERNAME:

PASSWORD(S):

NOTES/SECURITY QUESTIONS/PINS:

WEBSITE:

EMAIL:

USERNAME:

PASSWORD(S):

NOTES/SECURITY QUESTIONS/PINS:

WEBSITE:

EMAIL:

USERNAME:

PASSWORD(S):

NOTES/SECURITY QUESTIONS/PINS:

WEBSITE:

EMAIL:

USERNAME:

PASSWORD(S):

NOTES/SECURITY QUESTIONS/PINS:

WEBSITE:

EMAIL:

USERNAME:

PASSWORD(S):

NOTES/SECURITY QUESTIONS/PINS:

WEBSITE:

EMAIL:

USERNAME:

PASSWORD(S):

NOTES/SECURITY QUESTIONS/PINS:

WEBSITE:

EMAIL:

USERNAME:

PASSWORD(S):

NOTES/SECURITY QUESTIONS/PINS:

WEBSITE:

EMAIL:

USERNAME:

PASSWORD(S):

NOTES/SECURITY QUESTIONS/PINS:

WEBSITE:

EMAIL:

USERNAME:

PASSWORD(S):

NOTES/SECURITY QUESTIONS/PINS:

WEBSITE:

EMAIL:

USERNAME:

PASSWORD(S):

n

NOTES/SECURITY QUESTIONS/PINS:

WEBSITE:

EMAIL:

USERNAME:

PASSWORD(S):

NOTES/SECURITY QUESTIONS/PINS:

WEBSITE:

EMAIL:

USERNAME:

PASSWORD(S):

NOTES/SECURITY QUESTIONS/PINS:

WEBSITE:

EMAIL:

USERNAME:

PASSWORD(S):

NOTES/SECURITY QUESTIONS/PINS:

WEBSITE:

EMAIL:

USERNAME:

PASSWORD(S):

NOTES/SECURITY QUESTIONS/PINS:

WEBSITE:

EMAIL:

USERNAME:

PASSWORD(S):

NOTES/SECURITY QUESTIONS/PINS:

WEBSITE:

EMAIL:

USERNAME:

PASSWORD(S):

n

NOTES/SECURITY QUESTIONS/PINS:

WEBSITE:

EMAIL:

USERNAME:

PASSWORD(S):

NOTES/SECURITY QUESTIONS/PINS:

WEBSITE:

EMAIL:

USERNAME:

PASSWORD(S):

NOTES/SECURITY QUESTIONS/PINS:

WEBSITE:

EMAIL:

USERNAME:

PASSWORD(S):

NOTES/SECURITY QUESTIONS/PINS:

WEBSITE:

EMAIL:

USERNAME:

PASSWORD(S):

NOTES/SECURITY QUESTIONS/PINS:

WEBSITE:

EMAIL:

USERNAME:

PASSWORD(S):

NOTES/SECURITY QUESTIONS/PINS:

WEBSITE:

EMAIL:

USERNAME:

PASSWORD(S):

NOTES/SECURITY QUESTIONS/PINS:

WEBSITE:

EMAIL:

USERNAME:

PASSWORD(S):

NOTES/SECURITY QUESTIONS/PINS:

WEBSITE:

EMAIL:

USERNAME:

PASSWORD(S):

NOTES/SECURITY QUESTIONS/PINS:

WEBSITE:

EMAIL:

USERNAME:

PASSWORD(S):

0

NOTES/SECURITY QUESTIONS/PINS:

WEBSITE:

EMAIL:

USERNAME:

PASSWORD(S):

NOTES/SECURITY QUESTIONS/PINS:

WEBSITE:

EMAIL:

USERNAME:

PASSWORD(S):

NOTES/SECURITY QUESTIONS/PINS:

WEBSITE:

EMAIL:

USERNAME:

PASSWORD(S):

NOTES/SECURITY QUESTIONS/PINS:

WEBSITE:

EMAIL:

USERNAME:

PASSWORD(S):

NOTES/SECURITY QUESTIONS/PINS:

WEBSITE:

EMAIL:

USERNAME:

PASSWORD(S):

NOTES/SECURITY QUESTIONS/PINS:

WEBSITE:

EMAIL:

USERNAME:

PASSWORD(S):

NOTES/SECURITY QUESTIONS/PINS:

WEBSITE:

EMAIL:

USERNAME:

PASSWORD(S):

NOTES/SECURITY QUESTIONS/PINS:

WEBSITE:

EMAIL:

USERNAME:

PASSWORD(S):

NOTES/SECURITY QUESTIONS/PINS:

WEBSITE:

EMAIL:

USERNAME:

PASSWORD(S):

P NOTES/SECURITY QUESTIONS/PINS:

WEBSITE:

EMAIL:

USERNAME:

PASSWORD(S):

NOTES/SECURITY QUESTIONS/PINS:

WEBSITE:

EMAIL:

USERNAME:

PASSWORD(S):

NOTES/SECURITY QUESTIONS/PINS:

WEBSITE:

EMAIL:

USERNAME:

PASSWORD(S):

NOTES/SECURITY QUESTIONS/PINS:

_P_

WEBSITE:

EMAIL:

USERNAME:

PASSWORD(S):

NOTES/SECURITY QUESTIONS/PINS:

WEBSITE:

EMAIL:

USERNAME:

PASSWORD(S):

NOTES/SECURITY QUESTIONS/PINS:

WEBSITE:

EMAIL:

USERNAME:

PASSWORD(S):

NOTES/SECURITY QUESTIONS/PINS:

WEBSITE:

EMAIL:

USERNAME:

PASSWORD(S):

NOTES/SECURITY QUESTIONS/PINS:

WEBSITE:

EMAIL:

USERNAME:

PASSWORD(S):

NOTES/SECURITY QUESTIONS/PINS:

WEBSITE:

EMAIL:

USERNAME:

PASSWORD(S):

NOTES/SECURITY QUESTIONS/PINS:

Q

WEBSITE:

EMAIL:

USERNAME:

PASSWORD(S):

NOTES/SECURITY QUESTIONS/PINS:

WEBSITE:

EMAIL:

USERNAME:

PASSWORD(S):

NOTES/SECURITY QUESTIONS/PINS:

WEBSITE:

EMAIL:

USERNAME:

PASSWORD(S):

NOTES/SECURITY QUESTIONS/PINS:

WEBSITE:

EMAIL:

USERNAME:

PASSWORD(S):

NOTES/SECURITY QUESTIONS/PINS:

WEBSITE:

EMAIL:

USERNAME:

PASSWORD(S):

NOTES/SECURITY QUESTIONS/PINS:

WEBSITE:

EMAIL:

USERNAME:

PASSWORD(S):

NOTES/SECURITY QUESTIONS/PINS:

WEBSITE:

EMAIL:

USERNAME:

PASSWORD(S):

NOTES/SECURITY QUESTIONS/PINS:

WEBSITE:

EMAIL:

USERNAME:

PASSWORD(S):

NOTES/SECURITY QUESTIONS/PINS:

WEBSITE:

EMAIL:

USERNAME:

PASSWORD(S):

NOTES/SECURITY QUESTIONS/PINS:

WEBSITE:

EMAIL:

USERNAME:

PASSWORD(S):

NOTES/SECURITY QUESTIONS/PINS:

WEBSITE:

EMAIL:

USERNAME:

PASSWORD(S):

NOTES/SECURITY QUESTIONS/PINS:

WEBSITE:

EMAIL:

USERNAME:

PASSWORD(S):

NOTES/SECURITY QUESTIONS/PINS:

R

WEBSITE:

EMAIL:

USERNAME:

PASSWORD(S):

NOTES/SECURITY QUESTIONS/PINS:

WEBSITE:

EMAIL:

USERNAME:

PASSWORD(S):

NOTES/SECURITY QUESTIONS/PINS:

WEBSITE:

EMAIL:

USERNAME:

PASSWORD(S):

NOTES/SECURITY QUESTIONS/PINS:

R

WEBSITE:

EMAIL:

USERNAME:

PASSWORD(S):

NOTES/SECURITY QUESTIONS/PINS:

WEBSITE:

EMAIL:

USERNAME:

PASSWORD(S):

NOTES/SECURITY QUESTIONS/PINS:

WEBSITE:

EMAIL:

USERNAME:

PASSWORD(S):

NOTES/SECURITY QUESTIONS/PINS:

WEBSITE:

EMAIL:

USERNAME:

PASSWORD(S):

NOTES/SECURITY QUESTIONS/PINS:

WEBSITE:

EMAIL:

USERNAME:

PASSWORD(S):

NOTES/SECURITY QUESTIONS/PINS:

WEBSITE:

EMAIL:

USERNAME:

PASSWORD(S):

NOTES/SECURITY QUESTIONS/PINS:

R

WEBSITE:

EMAIL:

USERNAME:

PASSWORD(S):

NOTES/SECURITY QUESTIONS/PINS:

WEBSITE:

EMAIL:

USERNAME:

PASSWORD(S):

NOTES/SECURITY QUESTIONS/PINS:

WEBSITE:

EMAIL:

USERNAME:

PASSWORD(S):

NOTES/SECURITY QUESTIONS/PINS:

WEBSITE:

EMAIL:

USERNAME:

PASSWORD(S):

NOTES/SECURITY QUESTIONS/PINS:

WEBSITE:

EMAIL:

USERNAME:

PASSWORD(S):

NOTES/SECURITY QUESTIONS/PINS:

WEBSITE:

EMAIL:

USERNAME:

PASSWORD(S):

NOTES/SECURITY QUESTIONS/PINS:

S

WEBSITE:

EMAIL:

USERNAME:

PASSWORD(S):

NOTES/SECURITY QUESTIONS/PINS:

WEBSITE:

EMAIL:

USERNAME:

PASSWORD(S):

NOTES/SECURITY QUESTIONS/PINS:

WEBSITE:

EMAIL:

USERNAME:

PASSWORD(S):

NOTES/SECURITY QUESTIONS/PINS:

5

WEBSITE:

EMAIL:

USERNAME:

PASSWORD(S):

NOTES/SECURITY QUESTIONS/PINS:

WEBSITE:

EMAIL:

USERNAME:

PASSWORD(S):

NOTES/SECURITY QUESTIONS/PINS:

WEBSITE:

EMAIL:

USERNAME:

PASSWORD(S):

NOTES/SECURITY QUESTIONS/PINS:

S

WEBSITE:

EMAIL:

USERNAME:

PASSWORD(S):

NOTES/SECURITY QUESTIONS/PINS:

WEBSITE:

EMAIL:

USERNAME:

PASSWORD(S):

NOTES/SECURITY QUESTIONS/PINS:

WEBSITE:

EMAIL:

USERNAME:

PASSWORD(S):

NOTES/SECURITY QUESTIONS/PINS:

WEBSITE:

EMAIL:

USERNAME:

PASSWORD(S):

NOTES/SECURITY QUESTIONS/PINS:

WEBSITE:

EMAIL:

USERNAME:

PASSWORD(S):

NOTES/SECURITY QUESTIONS/PINS:

WEBSITE:

EMAIL:

USERNAME:

PASSWORD(S):

NOTES/SECURITY QUESTIONS/PINS:

WEBSITE:

EMAIL:

USERNAME:

PASSWORD(S):

NOTES/SECURITY QUESTIONS/PINS:

WEBSITE:

EMAIL:

USERNAME:

PASSWORD(S):

NOTES/SECURITY QUESTIONS/PINS:

WEBSITE:

EMAIL:

USERNAME:

PASSWORD(S):

NOTES/SECURITY QUESTIONS/PINS:

WEBSITE:

EMAIL:

USERNAME:

PASSWORD(S):

NOTES/SECURITY QUESTIONS/PINS:

WEBSITE:

EMAIL:

USERNAME:

PASSWORD(S):

NOTES/SECURITY QUESTIONS/PINS:

WEBSITE:

EMAIL:

USERNAME:

PASSWORD(S):

NOTES/SECURITY QUESTIONS/PINS:

WEBSITE:

EMAIL:

USERNAME:

PASSWORD(S):

NOTES/SECURITY QUESTIONS/PINS:

WEBSITE:

EMAIL:

USERNAME:

PASSWORD(S):

_____

_____

NOTES/SECURITY QUESTIONS/PINS:

_____

_____

WEBSITE:

EMAIL:

USERNAME:

PASSWORD(S):

_____

_____

NOTES/SECURITY QUESTIONS/PINS:

_____

_____

_____

WEBSITE:

EMAIL:

USERNAME:

PASSWORD(S):

_____

_____

NOTES/SECURITY QUESTIONS/PINS:

_____

_____

WEBSITE:

EMAIL:

USERNAME:

PASSWORD(S):

NOTES/SECURITY QUESTIONS/PINS:

WEBSITE:

EMAIL:

USERNAME:

PASSWORD(S):

NOTES/SECURITY QUESTIONS/PINS:

WEBSITE:

EMAIL:

USERNAME:

PASSWORD(S):

NOTES/SECURITY QUESTIONS/PINS:

WEBSITE:

EMAIL:

USERNAME:

PASSWORD(S):

NOTES/SECURITY QUESTIONS/PINS:

WEBSITE:

EMAIL:

USERNAME:

PASSWORD(S):

NOTES/SECURITY QUESTIONS/PINS:

WEBSITE:

EMAIL:

USERNAME:

PASSWORD(S):

NOTES/SECURITY QUESTIONS/PINS:

WEBSITE:

EMAIL:

USERNAME:

PASSWORD(S):

_____

_____

NOTES/SECURITY QUESTIONS/PINS:

_____

_____

WEBSITE:

EMAIL:

USERNAME:

PASSWORD(S):

_____

_____

NOTES/SECURITY QUESTIONS/PINS:

_____

_____

WEBSITE:

u EMAIL:

USERNAME:

PASSWORD(S):

_____

_____

NOTES/SECURITY QUESTIONS/PINS:

_____

_____

WEBSITE:

EMAIL:

USERNAME:

PASSWORD(S):

NOTES/SECURITY QUESTIONS/PINS:

WEBSITE:

EMAIL:

USERNAME:

PASSWORD(S):

NOTES/SECURITY QUESTIONS/PINS:

WEBSITE:

EMAIL:

USERNAME:

PASSWORD(S):

NOTES/SECURITY QUESTIONS/PINS:

WEBSITE:

EMAIL:

USERNAME:

PASSWORD(S):

NOTES/SECURITY QUESTIONS/PINS:

WEBSITE:

EMAIL:

USERNAME:

PASSWORD(S):

NOTES/SECURITY QUESTIONS/PINS:

WEBSITE:

EMAIL:

USERNAME:

PASSWORD(S):

NOTES/SECURITY QUESTIONS/PINS:

WEBSITE:

EMAIL:

USERNAME:

PASSWORD(S):

NOTES/SECURITY QUESTIONS/PINS:

WEBSITE:

EMAIL:

USERNAME:

PASSWORD(S):

NOTES/SECURITY QUESTIONS/PINS:

WEBSITE:

EMAIL:

USERNAME:

PASSWORD(S):

NOTES/SECURITY QUESTIONS/PINS:

WEBSITE:

EMAIL:

USERNAME:

PASSWORD(S):

NOTES/SECURITY QUESTIONS/PINS:

WEBSITE:

EMAIL:

USERNAME:

PASSWORD(S):

NOTES/SECURITY QUESTIONS/PINS:

WEBSITE:

EMAIL:

USERNAME:

PASSWORD(S):

NOTES/SECURITY QUESTIONS/PINS:

WEBSITE:

EMAIL:

USERNAME:

PASSWORD(S):

_____

_____

NOTES/SECURITY QUESTIONS/PINS:

_____

_____

WEBSITE:

EMAIL:

USERNAME:

PASSWORD(S):

_____

_____

NOTES/SECURITY QUESTIONS/PINS:

_____

_____

WEBSITE:

EMAIL:

USERNAME:

PASSWORD(S):

_____

_____

NOTES/SECURITY QUESTIONS/PINS:

_____

_____

WEBSITE:

EMAIL:

USERNAME:

PASSWORD(S):

NOTES/SECURITY QUESTIONS/PINS:

WEBSITE:

EMAIL:

USERNAME:

PASSWORD(S):

NOTES/SECURITY QUESTIONS/PINS:

WEBSITE:

EMAIL:

USERNAME:

PASSWORD(S):

NOTES/SECURITY QUESTIONS/PINS:

WEBSITE:

EMAIL:

USERNAME:

PASSWORD(S):

NOTES/SECURITY QUESTIONS/PINS:

WEBSITE:

EMAIL:

USERNAME:

PASSWORD(S):

NOTES/SECURITY QUESTIONS/PINS:

WEBSITE:

EMAIL:

USERNAME:

PASSWORD(S):

NOTES/SECURITY QUESTIONS/PINS:

WEBSITE:

EMAIL:

USERNAME:

PASSWORD(S):

NOTES/SECURITY QUESTIONS/PINS:

WEBSITE:

EMAIL:

USERNAME:

PASSWORD(S):

NOTES/SECURITY QUESTIONS/PINS:

WEBSITE:

EMAIL:

USERNAME:

PASSWORD(S):

NOTES/SECURITY QUESTIONS/PINS:

WEBSITE:

EMAIL:

USERNAME:

PASSWORD(S):

NOTES/SECURITY QUESTIONS/PINS:

WEBSITE:

EMAIL:

USERNAME:

PASSWORD(S):

NOTES/SECURITY QUESTIONS/PINS:

WEBSITE:

EMAIL:

USERNAME:

PASSWORD(S):

NOTES/SECURITY QUESTIONS/PINS:

WEBSITE:

EMAIL:

USERNAME:

PASSWORD(S):

NOTES/SECURITY QUESTIONS/PINS:

WEBSITE:

EMAIL:

USERNAME:

PASSWORD(S):

NOTES/SECURITY QUESTIONS/PINS:

WEBSITE:

EMAIL:

USERNAME:

PASSWORD(S):

X

NOTES/SECURITY QUESTIONS/PINS:

WEBSITE:

EMAIL:

USERNAME:

PASSWORD(S):

NOTES/SECURITY QUESTIONS/PINS:

WEBSITE:

EMAIL:

USERNAME:

PASSWORD(S):

NOTES/SECURITY QUESTIONS/PINS:

WEBSITE:

EMAIL:

USERNAME:

PASSWORD(S):

NOTES/SECURITY QUESTIONS/PINS:

WEBSITE:

EMAIL:

USERNAME:

PASSWORD(S):

NOTES/SECURITY QUESTIONS/PINS:

WEBSITE:

EMAIL:

USERNAME:

PASSWORD(S):

NOTES/SECURITY QUESTIONS/PINS:

WEBSITE:

EMAIL:

USERNAME:

PASSWORD(S):

NOTES/SECURITY QUESTIONS/PINS:

WEBSITE:

EMAIL:

USERNAME:

PASSWORD(S):

NOTES/SECURITY QUESTIONS/PINS:

WEBSITE:

EMAIL:

USERNAME:

PASSWORD(S):

NOTES/SECURITY QUESTIONS/PINS:

WEBSITE:

EMAIL:

USERNAME:

PASSWORD(S):

y

NOTES/SECURITY QUESTIONS/PINS:

WEBSITE:

EMAIL:

USERNAME:

PASSWORD(S):

NOTES/SECURITY QUESTIONS/PINS:

WEBSITE:

EMAIL:

USERNAME:

PASSWORD(S):

NOTES/SECURITY QUESTIONS/PINS:

WEBSITE:

EMAIL:

USERNAME:

PASSWORD(S):

NOTES/SECURITY QUESTIONS/PINS:

WEBSITE:

EMAIL:

USERNAME:

PASSWORD(S):

NOTES/SECURITY QUESTIONS/PINS:

WEBSITE:

EMAIL:

USERNAME:

PASSWORD(S):

NOTES/SECURITY QUESTIONS/PINS:

WEBSITE:

EMAIL:

USERNAME:

PASSWORD(S):

NOTES/SECURITY QUESTIONS/PINS:

WEBSITE:

EMAIL:

USERNAME:

PASSWORD(S):

NOTES/SECURITY QUESTIONS/PINS:

WEBSITE:

EMAIL:

USERNAME:

PASSWORD(S):

NOTES/SECURITY QUESTIONS/PINS:

WEBSITE:

EMAIL:

USERNAME:

PASSWORD(S):

y

NOTES/SECURITY QUESTIONS/PINS:

WEBSITE:

EMAIL:

USERNAME:

PASSWORD(S):

NOTES/SECURITY QUESTIONS/PINS:

WEBSITE:

EMAIL:

USERNAME:

PASSWORD(S):

NOTES/SECURITY QUESTIONS/PINS:

WEBSITE:

EMAIL:

USERNAME:

PASSWORD(S):

NOTES/SECURITY QUESTIONS/PINS:

WEBSITE:

EMAIL:

USERNAME:

PASSWORD(S):

NOTES/SECURITY QUESTIONS/PINS:

WEBSITE:

EMAIL:

USERNAME:

PASSWORD(S):

NOTES/SECURITY QUESTIONS/PINS:

WEBSITE:

EMAIL:

USERNAME:

PASSWORD(S):

NOTES/SECURITY QUESTIONS/PINS:

WEBSITE:

EMAIL:

USERNAME:

PASSWORD(S):

NOTES/SECURITY QUESTIONS/PINS:

WEBSITE:

EMAIL:

USERNAME:

PASSWORD(S):

NOTES/SECURITY QUESTIONS/PINS:

WEBSITE:

EMAIL:

USERNAME:

PASSWORD(S):

NOTES/SECURITY QUESTIONS/PINS:

WEBSITE:

EMAIL:

USERNAME:

PASSWORD(S):

NOTES/SECURITY QUESTIONS/PINS:

WEBSITE:

EMAIL:

USERNAME:

PASSWORD(S):

NOTES/SECURITY QUESTIONS/PINS:

WEBSITE:

EMAIL:

USERNAME:

PASSWORD(S):

NOTES/SECURITY QUESTIONS/PINS:

WEBSITE:

EMAIL:

USERNAME:

PASSWORD(S):

NOTES/SECURITY QUESTIONS/PINS:

WEBSITE:

EMAIL:

USERNAME:

PASSWORD(S):

NOTES/SECURITY QUESTIONS/PINS:

WEBSITE:

EMAIL:

USERNAME:

PASSWORD(S):

NOTES/SECURITY QUESTIONS/PINS:

WEBSITE:

EMAIL:

USERNAME:

PASSWORD(S):

NOTES/SECURITY QUESTIONS/PINS:

WEBSITE:

EMAIL:

USERNAME:

PASSWORD(S):

NOTES/SECURITY QUESTIONS/PINS:

WEBSITE:

EMAIL:

USERNAME:

PASSWORD(S):

NOTES/SECURITY QUESTIONS/PINS:

WEBSITE:

EMAIL:

USERNAME:

PASSWORD(S):

NOTES/SECURITY QUESTIONS/PINS:

WEBSITE:

EMAIL:

USERNAME:

PASSWORD(S):

NOTES/SECURITY QUESTIONS/PINS:

WEBSITE:

EMAIL:

USERNAME:

PASSWORD(S):

NOTES/SECURITY QUESTIONS/PINS:

WEBSITE:

EMAIL:

USERNAME:

PASSWORD(S):

NOTES/SECURITY QUESTIONS/PINS:

WEBSITE:

EMAIL:

USERNAME:

PASSWORD(S):

NOTES/SECURITY QUESTIONS/PINS:

WEBSITE:

EMAIL:

USERNAME:

PASSWORD(S):

NOTES/SECURITY QUESTIONS/PINS: